PARIS

THE CITY AT A GLANCE

Tour Montparnasse
Looming over low-rise Paris, the 210m-high
1970s landmark is back in fashion once again.
See p012

Musée d'Orsay
Housed in Victor Laloux's 1900 Gare d'Orsay
and always thronged, this emblem of old Paris
has works by Rodin, Manet and Renoir.
1 rue de la Légion d'Honneur, 7ᵉ, T 40 49 48 14

Palais Garnier
Charles Garnier's ornate Second Empire
monument boasts an eight-tonne crystal
chandelier (that crushed an opera-goer in
1896) and Marc Chagall's 1964 ceiling ar
8 rue Scribe, 9ᵉ, T 08 92 89 90 90

D0921298

Jardin des Tuileries
In the riverside gardens connecting the Louvre
(see p028) and place de la Concorde, the Jeu
de Paume gallery (1 place de la Concorde, 8ᵉ,
T 47 03 12 50) shows world-class photography.

Hôtel des Invalides
Now a military museum, this former soldiers'
hospice and convent, which dates from 1674,
was modified to house Napoleon Bonaparte's
superbly grand tomb, located under the dome.
Esplanade des Invalides, 7ᵉ, T 08 10 11 33 99

Eglise de la Trinité
Théodore Ballu's 1867 church was part of the
reorganisation of Paris under Haussmann.
Place d'Estienne d'Orves, 9ᵉ, T 48 74 12 77

Grand Palais
The vast glass-roofed exhibition hall built for
the 1900 Expo hosts art fairs including FIAC
and Monumenta, which lives up to its name.
*3 avenue du Général Eisenhower, 8ᵉ,
T 44 13 17 17*

INTRODUCTION
THE CHANGING FACE OF THE URBAN SCENE

It can be tempting to get nostalgic about Paris, to imagine there is still a corner where you'll catch a glimpse of Eugène de Rastignac, or stumble across a beatific Miles Davis en route to Club Saint-Germain. Yet, defying those who believe it to be nothing more than a beguiling relic, Paris surges ahead with major cultural projects, as fast-moving and trend-driven as any other digital-age capital.

Montmartre, recently fashionable, has settled into a gentrified calm, although it is still a dream for shopping and sightseeing. The *branché* district right now, where contemporary design spaces and independent boutiques cluster, is the Haut-Marais, especially the northern fringes and up into the 10th around post-seedy rue du Faubourg Saint-Denis. The 11th, known for grungy nightlife, has become a hive of gastro innovation. Eventually, you may prefer to retire from the bobo bustle to more tranquil areas such as the 5th, the leafy 7th, and the bourgeois galleries of Saint-Germain. Equally good for slowing the pace are the fashion flagships and elite hotels and restaurants lining the wealthy boulevards of the Right Bank.

Plans for Le Grand Paris, a hugely ambitious extension of the tightly belted core, will see more change here than at any time since Haussmann, with large-scale urban projects undertaken, and the heart of the metropolis redesignated as one of several centres. For now, while you can still walk from the Eiffel Tower to place de la Bastille and feel you've seen this elegant city, classic Paris lives.

ESSENTIAL INFO
FACTS, FIGURES AND USEFUL ADDRESSES

TOURIST OFFICE
25 rue des Pyramides, 1er
www.parisinfo.com

TRANSPORT
Airport transfer to city centre
RER line B trains depart regularly from
Charles de Gaulle Airport between 5am and
12am. The journey takes 25 to 35 minutes
www.aeroportsdeparis.fr
Car hire
Avis
T 08 21 23 07 60
www.avis.fr
Metro
Trains run from 5.30am until 1am, Sunday
to Thursday; and from 5.30am until 2am
on Fridays and Saturdays
www.ratp.fr
Taxi
Taxis G7
www.taxig7.fr
Travel Card
A carnet (10 metro/bus tickets) is €14.10

EMERGENCY SERVICES
Emergencies
T 112
24-hour pharmacy
Pharmacie Les Champs Dhéry
84 avenue des Champs-Élysées, 8e
T 45 62 02 41

EMBASSIES
British Embassy
35 rue du Faubourg Saint-Honoré, 8e
T 44 51 31 00
www.gov.uk/government/world/france
US Embassy
4 avenue Gabriel, 8e
T 43 12 22 22
france.usembassy.gov

POSTAL SERVICES
Post office
52 rue du Louvre, 1er
T 40 28 21 51
Shipping
UPS
T 08 21 23 38 77
www.ups.com

BOOKS
Le Corbusier: Ideas & Forms
by William J R Curtis (Phaidon)
Paris: de la Rue à la Galerie by Nicolas
Chenus and Samantha Longhi (Pyramyd)

WEBSITES
Art/Design
www.musee-orsay.fr
www.patrickseguin.com
Newspaper
www.lemonde.fr

EVENTS
Art Paris
www.artparis.fr
Maison & Objet
www.maison-objet.com
Nuit Blanche
www.quefaire.paris.fr/nuitblanche

COST OF LIVING
**Taxi from Charles de Gaulle Airport
to city centre**
€50
Cappuccino
€4
Packet of cigarettes
€6
Daily newspaper
€2
Bottle of champagne
€80

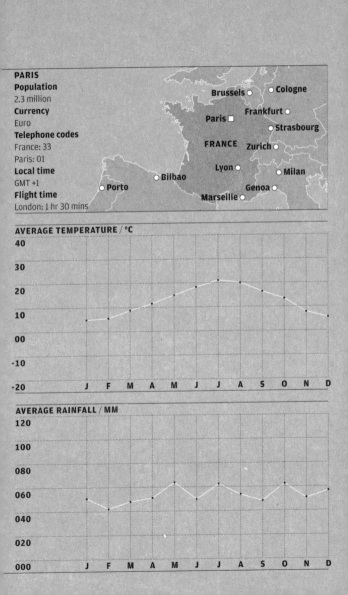

PARIS
Population
2.3 million
Currency
Euro
Telephone codes
France: 33
Paris: 01
Local time
GMT +1
Flight time
London: 1 hr 30 mins

Brussels ○   ○ Cologne
                Frankfurt ○
Paris □
                ○ Strasbourg
FRANCE Zurich ○
Lyon ○   ○ Milan
○ Bilbao
                Genoa ○
Marseille ○
○ Porto

AVERAGE TEMPERATURE / °C

40
30
20
10
00
-10
-20
   J F M A M J J A S O N D

AVERAGE RAINFALL / MM

120
100
080
060
040
020
000
   J F M A M J J A S O N D

NEIGHBOURHOODS

THE AREAS YOU NEED TO KNOW AND WHY

To help you navigate the city, we've chosen the most interesting districts (see below and the map inside the back cover) and colour-coded our featured venues, according to their location; those venues that are outside these areas are not coloured.

MONTMARTRE/PIGALLE

Rising above the city, Montmartre remains aloof from the rest of Paris. Check into the tranquil Hôtel Particulier (see p021) and explore the cafés and restaurants that line rue des Martyrs. Pigalle is up-and-coming. Make a reservation for dinner at modern bistrot Le Pantruche (see p042).

CANAL SAINT-MARTIN

The east-Paris bobo (*bourgeois-bohème*) crowd lingers beside the banks of this canal, along rue de Marseille and rue Beaurepaire. Stay at Le Citizen (96 quai de Jemmapes, 10e, T 83 62 55 50) for its watery views. To the east, in the 19th, the hipsters continue to push into Belleville.

CHAMPS-ÉLYSÉES

There is a slight stain of tackiness around the Champs-Élysées itself, but the area still has plenty to offer, including Pavillon Ledoyen (see p032), now the domain of Yannick Alléno, and contemporary luxury hotels such as La Maison Champs Élysées (8 rue Jean Goujon, 8e, T 40 74 64 65).

RÉPUBLIQUE/BASTILLE

Rue Oberkampf's nightlife is not what it was, but the area has scrubbed up nicely, as bars like Le Perchoir (see p024) lure revellers. Thanks to Iñaki Aizpitarte of Le Châteaubriand (see p032), Taku Sekine's Dersou (see p036) and Bertrand Grébaut's Septime (see p052), the border of the 11th and the 12th is now a hot culinary zone.

MARAIS

Art galleries and fashion boutiques, such as Galerie Perrotin (76 rue de Turenne, 3e, T 42 16 79 79) and Études (see p082), are dotted around rue Debelleyme, rue de Saintonge and rue Charlot. At the northern edge, don't miss avant-garde stores The Broken Arm (see p025) and Ofr (see p080).

BEAUBOURG/LOUVRE

The Louvre (see p028) is an essential stop, despite its spirit-sapping vastness and the Dan Brown-devouring hordes. Don't miss out on its 2012 Department of Islamic Art, followed by lunch nearby at no-bookings udon noodle specialist Kunitoraya (5 rue Villedo, 1er, T 47 03 07 74).

SAINT-GERMAIN/QUARTIER LATIN

This smart neighbourhood is packed with galleries, cafés and shops, notably swish department store Le Bon Marché (24 rue de Sèvres, 7e, T 44 39 80 00) and the high-design Hermès Sèvres (see p080), set in an art deco former indoor swimming pool; stop off at its Le Plongeoir tearoom.

LES INVALIDES

Already lined with imposing monuments, this district can now boast Jean Nouvel's Musée du quai Branly (see p024); compare and contrast with the *quartier*'s former highlight, the UNESCO Headquarters (see p014). Feast and then rest at Thoumieux (see p039), which consists of a splendid brasserie, restaurant and boutique hotel.

LANDMARKS
THE SHAPE OF THE CITY SKYLINE

Unlike Rome or Venice, Paris never has to live off its past for very long, because it always manages to reinvent itself. How it does this has a lot to do with the structure of the metropolis. It has retained its basic shape for centuries by spreading out steadily from the diminutive island in the river, Île de la Cité, where the Parisii, a community of Celtic fisherfolk, settled in 250BC. As its population increased, the city expanded in concentric circles, now stretching as far as the Périphérique ring road. Chloé-clad commuters lead *Desperate Housewives*-on-the-Seine lifestyles in the leafy western suburbs, such as Saint-Cloud and Neuilly, while the underclass re-enacts *La Haine* in 1950s hellholes beyond the ring road.

Contemporary Paris consists of more than two million people living inside the 9.7km diameter of the Périphérique, with Île de la Cité still at its centre. The good news is that, whereas sprawling urban nodes such as LA can afford to neglect their architecture, land is so precious within the unofficial boundary of the French capital that Parisians strive to preserve theirs. And ever since Henri IV ordered the creation of a chichi residential district, the Marais, around place des Vosges in the early 1600s, the municipality has put almost as much effort into building new monuments as it has into cherishing old ones. All of which means that not only is navigation easy, but the landmarks that line the way are worth lingering over. *For full addresses, see Resources.*

Centre Pompidou

The moment when architecture became icon can be traced to 1977, when Richard Rogers, Renzo Piano and Gianfranco Franchini's technical and functional tour de force was unveiled. The Pompidou can appear untidy, but it is a classic example of a building as city symbol. It houses the Musée National d'Art Moderne, a library and a musical research centre. Seven storeys of glass, steel and concrete are encased in an exoskeleton of colour-coded pipes – green for plumbing, blue for internal climate control, yellow for electrics, and red for communication. In 2010, the Pompidou opened an outpost in Metz (T 03 87 15 39 39). With the bar for its design set almost impossibly high, Shigeru Ban and Jean de Gastines came up with a hexagonal plan enveloped in an undulating marquee-style wood roof. *Place Georges Pompidou, 4ᵉ, T 44 78 12 33, www.centrepompidou.fr*

Tour Montparnasse

The redevelopment of the down-at-heel area around Gare Montparnasse in the early 1960s was, by and large, a piece of inspired city planning. Jean Dubuisson's scheme included a monumental slab of a residential block, with a wonderful gridded curtain wall. Unfortunately, it also allowed for this 210m-tall totem pole in the middle of low-rise Paris. Together with the high-rise buildings along the Seine, which were commissioned under Georges Pompidou's prime ministership, this tower, finished in 1973, is back in vogue with city opinion-formers. On the 56th floor, there is an observation terrace, a champagne bar and a glamorous restaurant, Ciel de Paris (T 40 64 77 64; reservations only) that is designed by Noé Duchaufour-Lawrance. *33 avenue du Maine, 15ᵉ, T 45 38 52 56, www.tourmontparnasse56.com*

Grande Arche de la Défense

The proposal to construct a new business district to the west of the centre was first advanced in the early 1950s, but it was this 1989 landmark that fixed La Défense in the popular imagination. The hollowed-out cube reaches up to 110m high, and the stark, almost graphic lines of its facades are emphasised by the use of glazing and white Carrara marble. The creation of a Danish pair, architect Johan Otto von Spreckelsen and engineer Erik Reitzel, the arch is scaled on both sides by lifts, which provide panoramic views of greater Paris, as well as down the axis of Champs-Élysées (the roof has been closed but is set to reopen in 2017). Nearby is Christian de Portzamparc's gleaming, angular Tour Granite, which was built for Groupe Société Générale and completed in 2008.

1 parvis de la Défense

UNESCO Headquarters

Conceived by celebrated architects Marcel Breuer, Bernard Zehrfuss and Pier Luigi Nervi, this complex was one of the first major modern works to be constructed in the centre of the city. When it was finished in 1958, writer Lewis Mumford dismissed it as a 'museum of antiquated modernities'. Even today, in the eyes of some critics, the building hasn't really recovered from this withering assessment. All the same, the seven-storey, Y-shaped office block (left), resting on 72 concrete stilts, has become a landmark, and the congress hall, with its concertina-like structure, is now thought of as a masterpiece of design. Picasso, Miró, Tàpies, Calder, Moore, Giacometti, Brassaï and Le Corbusier were just some of the artists commissioned to create pieces for the site; in 1995, the Japanese architect Tadao Ando added an exquisite small meditation space to the ensemble. *7 place de Fontenoy, 7ᵉ, www.unesco.org*

HOTELS

WHERE TO STAY AND WHICH ROOMS TO BOOK

The deluxe room count in Paris, one of the world's great hotel cities, just keeps rising. Over the past few years, big-hitting Asian brands like Mandarin Oriental, Shangri-La and Peninsula (see p020) have joined the grandes dames; Plaza Athénée (25 avenue Montaigne, 8e, T 53 67 66 65) has quietly acquired a new wing to compete, and architect Thierry Despont has cleverly transformed the storied Ritz (15 place Vendôme, 1er, T 43 16 30 30), which relaunched in 2016.

Beyond the bells and whistles, attractive choices are appearing in upcoming areas. Hôtel Paradis (41 rue des Petites Écuries, 10e, T 45 23 08 22) has decor by Dorothée Meilichzon, and Hôtel Edgar (31 rue d'Alexandrie, 2e, T 40 41 05 19) has rooms created by an arty coterie and a decent seafood bistro. Cosy, boho Hôtel Providence (90 rue René Boulanger, 10e, T 46 34 34 04) is a food-led berth near a cool stretch of Strasbourg Saint-Denis. Another gourmet choice is Hôtel de Nell (7-9 rue du Conservatoire, 9e, T 44 83 83 60), due to its celebrated restaurant La Régalade Conservatoire.

There is minimalist cool in the 20th at Philippe Starck's Mama Shelter (109 rue de Bagnolet, 20e, T 43 48 48 48); in the Marais, the modish but not overweeningly hip Jules & Jim (11 rue des Gravilliers, 3e, T 44 54 13 13) remains a favourite. Out in the 16th, calm, understated rooms and a sensational outdoor pool at Hotel Molitor (13 rue Nungesser et Coli, 16e, T 56 07 08 50) are the draw. *For full addresses and room rates, see Resources.*

Hôtel Bachaumont

The 2015 arrival of this hotel, coupled with its neighbour, Nose perfumery (see p089), heralded an upmarket shift in the *quartier* around rue Montorgueil. Interior designer du jour Dorothée Meilichzon has returned this 1920s property to former glory (lobby, above), retaining the art deco mouldings, grand arches and Carrara marble floors. Similar motifs adorn the furnishings in the rooms, washed mainly in greys and blues, which range from petite to loft-like; opt for the airy Montmartre Suite, which has its own terrace. However, it is the restaurant (T 81 66 47 50), serving classic bistro fare (no share plates here), and Night Flight bar (T 48 58 56 23), where the gin-based Fennel Collins is a hit, that give Bachaumont most of its cred, and both are regularly packed. *18 rue Bachaumont, 2ᵉ, T 81 66 47 00, www.hotelbachaumont.com*

Amastan

In a quiet setting off rue du Faubourg Saint-Honoré, this boutique hotel, which opened in 2016, is a fresh choice in the well-heeled 8th. Designed by NOCC, the 24 rooms (double, pictured) are swathed in herringbone and have lacquered oak furniture, and accents of copper. The happening bar, Anouk, is festooned with plant life, and serves inventive cocktails.
34 rue Jean Mermoz, 8ᵉ, T 49 52 99 70

The Peninsula

Stupendously retooled for the 21st century, this historic pile glitters with hand-applied gold leaf and gleams with marble. Hoping to lure and secure China's new tourist class, The Peninsula serves congee alongside the croissants at breakfast, and the lavish LiLi restaurant (T 58 12 67 50) presents Sichuan and Cantonese dishes beneath giant silk tassels. The rooms are low-key, particularly considering the luxe elsewhere, featuring leather art deco-style headboards crafted by London artist Helen Murray, offset by high-tech lighting, entertainment run by tablet, and marble-clad bathrooms. The Historical Suite (above) has high ceilings and views over the Arc de Triomphe. The produce-led French cuisine at L'Oiseau Blanc (T 58 12 67 30) is perfectly pitched. *19 avenue Kléber, 16e, T 58 12 28 88, paris.peninsula.com*

Hôtel Particulier Montmartre

Despite the swarms of tourists en route to Sacré-Coeur, and the area's slow but steady gentrification, pockets of the Montmartre district retain an atmosphere unmatched anywhere else in Paris. On stylish avenue Junot, the discreet Particulier occupies a 19th-century townhouse, once owned by the Hermès family, and looks on to gardens by Louis Benech. The filmmaker Morgane Rousseau turned it into a five-suite hotel with a cinematic theme that incorporates works by French artists; reserve Poèmes et Chapeaux, a tribute to Olivier Saillard, or the Rideau de Cheveux Suite, which features photography by Natacha Lesueur. The hotel bar, Le Très Particulier, serves exquisite cocktails; house specialities use organic honey and herbs grown on-site.
23 avenue Junot, 18e, T 53 41 81 40, www.hotel-particulier-montmartre.com

Le Pigalle

This hotel is situated in a particularly hip pocket of Pigalle, which is known as SoPi in certain circles. It has a hyper-local ethos; art books are supplied by neighbourhood store Les Arpenteurs (T 53 16 47 96), the textiles are by Rue Hérold (see p086) and the ground-floor café/restaurant serves an all-day menu courtesy of gourmand hero Camille Fourmont, who helms La Buvette (see p048). Interiors, by Paris-based firm Festen (see p054), are an eclectic mix, with a certain retro charm that extends to the lounge (opposite) and rooms – Pigalle 21 (above) has a leather-upholstered bar. Nearby, the Grand Pigalle Hotel (T 85 73 12 00) also draws a chic crowd. Here, Italian chef Giovanni Passerini mans the kitchen, and the decor is by Dorothée Meilichzon. *9 rue Frochot, 9e, T 48 78 37 14, www.lepigalle.paris*

24 HOURS
SEE THE BEST OF THE CITY IN JUST ONE DAY

Owing to Paris' petite size relative to, say, London, the city smiles on intrepid visitors who want to explore both sides of the Seine. For brunch at weekends, try the anglophile affair at Le Bal Café (6 impasse de la Défense, 18e, T 44 70 75 51), the anything-goes menu at The Peninsula (see p020) or, for hot chocolate, champagne and madeleines, the Sunday spread at Un Dimanche à Paris (4 cour du Commerce Saint-André, 6e, T 56 81 18 18). Alternatively, a gourmet outing could well start on rue des Martyrs, winding down from Montmartre; pause for *lèche-vitrine* at Pâtisserie des Martyrs (No 22, 9e, T 71 18 24 70) and continue on rue du Faubourg-Montmartre for food shopping around Montorgueil. You could then go west to the Bois de Boulogne, for lunch by the pool at Molitor (see p016), followed by a look at Fondation Louis Vuitton (see p060), just one of the art behemoths on the must-see list, which includes Musée du quai Branly (37 quai Branly, 7e, T 56 61 70 00) on the Left Bank, and the raw spaces of Palais de Tokyo (see p026) across the river.

Much of what's exciting at night is concentrated around Bastille, Oberkampf and Ménilmontant, so head east for drinks *en plein air* at Le Perchoir (14 rue Crespin du Gast, 11e, T 48 06 18 48), or for a lively dinner at Aux Deux Amis (45 rue Oberkampf, 11e, T 58 30 38 13), which heaves with 30-somethings on Friday nights. After hours, the nightclub at Les Bains (see p046) has its groove back. *For full addresses, see Resources.*

11.00 The Broken Arm

The young Parisian trio behind hyper-hip concept store The Broken Arm struck gold when they secured this site in a historic residential building with a leafy outlook onto square du Temple. The two-storey boutique purveys a street-smart mix of clothing that captures (and influences) the zeitgeist, avant-garde accessories and a collection of smart magazines. Having championed fledgling local labels like Jacquemus and Vetements since inception, they've recently added more established names, including Céline, Balenciaga and Loewe, to the fold. The sunny corner café, where chef Linda Granebring serves up a relaxed but sophisticated breakfast and lunch menu, such as crab salad with raw broccoli and lemon, is the cherry on top.
12 rue Perrée, 3e, T 44 61 53 60, www.the-broken-arm.com

13.30 Palais de Tokyo

Extended in 2012, so it now reaches down to the Seine, Palais de Tokyo is a must for its surveys of contemporary art, and its architecture – a 22,000 sq m labyrinth of concrete chambers and lofty alcoves. Anne Lacaton and Jean-Philippe Vassal took a minimalist approach to the renovation, freeing up space and revealing the vast proportions. In some of the rooms, it can feel as if you're entering a no-go area, so unsignposted and unrefined is the finish. As many of the artworks are disruptive of normative seeing, the experience can be thrillingly disorienting; the venue's fabric is also subject to intervention. Afterwards have lunch at Monsieur Blue (above; T 47 20 90 47), designed by Joseph Dirand. The museum opens at noon; closed Tuesdays. *13 avenue du Président Wilson, 16e, T 81 97 35 88, www.palaisdetokyo.com*

16.00 Department of Islamic Art
The undulating roof of 2,350 triangular panels in gold and silver aluminium mesh that occupies Cour Visconti shields the Louvre's Islamic art treasures. Inaugurated in 2012, the structure has a deliberately cloak-like quality that saves it from what architect Mario Bellini, who designed the gallery with Rudy Ricciotti, says would have been 'embarrassing cross-pollination with the 18th-century character of the palace'. The illusion of suspension and fluidity gives the project a lightness and unexpectedness entirely in keeping with the museum's prior contemporary flourish, IM Pei's 1989 glass pyramid. The Islamic collection spans 1,300 years and three continents, covering ceramics, glassware, textiles, calligraphy and precious metals.
Louvre, 1 place du Carrousel, 1ᵉʳ, T 40 20 53 17, www.louvre.fr

19.30 Clover

This bistro by chef Jean-François Piège, once of Brasserie Thoumieux (see p039), is a detour from the white-tableclothed dining rooms he's accustomed, such as his exquisite Le Grand Restaurant (T 53 05 00 00) in the 8th, which opened in 2015. Clover is slender and convivial, not least because of the unusual interior set-up by Charlotte Biltgen that fully incorporates the kitchen into the dining room, as if you were at a dinner party. You'll find the Left Bank creative set seated on a tan leather banquette amid cedar shingle panelling, cracked Japanese raku wall tiles and retro light fixtures by Vilhelm Lauritzen. It's unpretentious, but the menu includes the kind of wizardry Piège is renowned for: beef seared on a paving stone, for example. *5 rue Perronet, 7e, T 75 50 00 05, www.clover-paris.com*

22.00 Gravity Bar

This stylish *cave à manger*, situated just off the Canal Saint-Martin, references the theme of extreme sports for its inventive, produce-driven cocktail menu. Mixologist Michael Mas, formerly of Le Mary Celeste (see p049), has conceived a list divided into four categories: Weightlessness, Cold Sweat, Disorientation and Overexcitement. The drinks themselves, though, cut through any gimmick: the Fruit du Passé combines herbal liqueurs, house-made celery syrup, lemon, liquorice powder and fennel seeds. Working predominantly with raw concrete and plywood, interior architect Antoine Vauclare fashioned the ceiling into a wave-like form that swoops over the circular bar. In the kitchen, chef Frédérick Boucher conjures up tapas-style small plates, like bonito tataki served with fresh orange.
44 rue des Vinaigriers, 10ᵉ, T 98 54 92 49

URBAN LIFE
CAFÉS, RESTAURANTS, BARS AND NIGHTCLUBS

The *bistronomie* scene that restored the city's culinary mettle is into its third decade, and Septime (see p052), Le Châteaubriand (129 avenue Parmentier, 11e, T 43 57 45 95) and Gregory Marchand's much-lauded Frenchie (5-6 rue du Nil, 2e, T 40 39 96 19) offer some of the most dynamic dining in Paris. Their alumni, such as Camille Fourmont (see p048), have since established their own informal, produce-savvy styles. Biodynamic and natural wines from small operations in France and Italy are the rule at these establishments.

At the high end, Yannick Alléno now shakes the pans at Pavillon Ledoyen (8 avenue Dutuit, 8e, T 53 05 10 01), and Pascal Barbot's Asian-tinged, veg-centric menu at L'Astrance (4 rue Beethoven, 16e, T 40 50 84 40) draws visiting chefs. The definitive bistro is arguably Paul Bert (18 rue Paul Bert, 11e, T 43 72 24 01), which has a seafood sibling next door, L'Ecailler du Bistrot (No 22, T 43 72 76 77).

Hot venues in the 11th – the must-visit arrondissement for food-lovers – include the casual Le Servan (32 rue Saint-Maur, 11e, T 55 28 51 82), run by ex-L'Astrance chef Tatiana Levha and her sister Katia, and Clown Bar (114 rue Amelot, 11e, T 43 55 87 35), the Saturne (see p053) team's takeover of a zany century-old annexe of the Cirque d'Hiver. In the Marais, SŌMA (13 rue de Saintonge, 3e, T 09 81 82 53 51) is a bustling *izakaya*. And the BBQ trend has arrived in Pigalle, at the aptly named Flesh (25 rue de Douai, 9e, T 42 81 21 93). *For full addresses, see Resources.*

52 Faubourg Saint Denis

Owner Charles Compagnon, also behind Le Richer (2 rue Richer) and L'Office (T 47 70 67 31), opened this neo-bistro in the heart of the buzzy Faubourg *quartier* in 2015, amid a fishmonger and string of kebab shops. A relaxed, modern all-dayer, it features raw, stripped-back interiors conceived by Vincent Eschalier and Gesa Hansen – a shell of polished concrete is warmed up by cognac-coloured leather booths, wood-veneer seating and jade-green tabletops. The menu lists light bistro fare with a twist: *oeuf mollet* with smoked eel, or burrata with pear and olive purée. There are no bookings (or phone number) so be prepared to wait. The lines are not as long at lunch, or drop in for an aperitif, as the inventive wine list is worth exploring.
52 rue du Faubourg Saint-Denis, 10e, www.faubourgstdenis.com

Ellsworth

Braden Perkins and Laura Adrian of Verjus (T 42 97 54 40) fame established sister restaurant Ellsworth to cater for the well-heeled lunch and Sunday brunch crowd (it opens all day but Verjus is dinner only). The buzzy bistro (opposite) – an understated mix of marble, oak, stone and brass – is slender but still feels spacious. From the kitchen, former Verjus chef Christopher Jankowski sends out seasonal dishes that showcase sustainability and whole-animal butchery (which is why pork, for example, might feature more than once), and simple, elegant small plates like *dorade* ceviche with radish, or fried violet artichoke with herb mayo. Book ahead or try your luck at the bar (above), designed by Phil Euell, and festooned with tidy rows of glassware. *34 rue de Richelieu, 1er, T 42 60 59 66, www.ellsworthparis.com*

Dersou
Helmed by chef Taku Sekine and cocktail whiz Amaury Guyot, Dersou has charmed locals with its inspired fusion menu and cocktail pairings. The space is gracefully sparse as any flourish is left to the plate: a dish of poached oysters and cauliflower cream is teamed with a bergamot-infused gin tipple. The Sunday brunch is one of the more original propositions in town.
21 rue Saint-Nicolas, 12°, T 09 81 01 12 73

Restaurant Guy Savoy

Arguably France's most lauded chef, Guy Savoy moved his three-Michelin-starred restaurant – housed for 28 years in a stark, modern site in the 17th – to the first floor of the grandiose Monnaie de Paris in 2015. Within the old French Mint, founded in 864 and reconstructed in the 18th century, the five dining rooms, each with soaring 3m-high windows, have been made over by Jean-Michel Wilmotte, and are awash with grey hues – contemporary artworks (by Pierre et Gilles, above) add extra panache. Colour is injected by handmade tableware with Joan Miró-style sketches by Virginia Mo, and the joyful, sublimely plated dishes, such as blue lobster 'raw-cooked' in cold steam, or artichoke and black truffle soup, served with a wild mushroom brioche. *Monnaie de Paris, 11 quai de Conti, 6e, T 43 80 40 61, www.guysavoy.com*

Brasserie Thoumieux

Since the relaunch by Thierry Costes, whose family is behind so many of Paris' see-and-be-seen destinations, this venue is abuzz again, offering a snapshot of the well-heeled habitués of the 7th. Amid red banquettes, orb lights, darkwood floors and room-length etched mirrors, chef Sylvestre Wahid delivers elevated bistro fare: beef tartare with sucrine hearts and crispy onion rings, *mi-cuit* (half-cooked) tuna steak, and an 'XXL' burger with *frites*. Sunday brunch consists of delicate baked goods, sourced from chic sister pâtisserie Gâteaux Thoumieux (T 45 51 12 12) over the road. Upstairs, restaurant Sylvestre (T 47 05 79 79) boasts two Michelin stars, and there is also a refined 14-room hotel (T 47 05 79 00) with interiors by India Mahdavi. *79 rue Saint-Dominique, 7ᵉ, T 47 05 79 00, www.thoumieux.fr*

Restaurant Yam'Tcha

The move to a spacious new venue on rue Saint-Honoré has seen Yam'Tcha rise to be one of the city's best fusion restaurants. The original spot (T 40 26 06 06), which is around the corner, focuses on bao buns and takeaway. Here, chef Adeline Grattard takes an upmarket approach. The multi-salon restaurant is flushed with tones of gold and green; the porcelain tableware, by Italian studio Potomak, adds a further splash of colour. It's a tranquil, gently lit space that matches the leisurely paced set menu, which might include red tuna served with bouchot mussels and sweet potato noodles, or langoustines with XO sauce. Enjoy with wine or ingenious tea pairings, prepared by Grattard's husband and resident tea master, Chiwah Chan. *121 rue Saint-Honoré, 1er, T 40 26 08 07, www.yamtcha.com*

Caillebotte

Parisians Franck Baranger, Edouard Bobin and Nicolas Chatellain followed up their wildly popular Pigalle bistro Le Pantruche (T 48 78 55 60) with this informal corner restaurant in the 9th arrondissement. On trend Nordic design notes – lightwood cladding and white marble tables – make this a refined lunch spot for well-heeled suits; it's more lively in the evenings, when the locals roll in. Inside, dark-turquoise banquettes add a sense of intimacy to the airy interiors. In the warmer months, try for a spot on the terrace. From the kitchen, Baranger turns out imaginative, seasonal three- and five-course set menus that he refreshes weekly; you might be served beef with potato millefeuille and garlic-parsley mousse, or langoustine with lychee and mango chutney. Closed at weekends.
8 rue Hippolyte Lebas, 9ᵉ, T 53 20 88 70

Café Oberkampf

Speciality coffee shops have spread like wildfire out from the Marais and into the 10th and 11th arrondissements. From Ten Belles (T 42 40 90 78) to Steel (T 06 47 58 32 46), Cream (T 09 83 66 58 43) and Boot (T 73 70 14 57), hip Parisians spend their weekends seeking out the best (and most Instagram-friendly) filter, Aeropress or cold brew. With a cute storefront, tucked behind the main boulevard, Oberkampf joined the café scene in 2015, serving top-notch blends – owner Guy Griffin rotates his bean supply among a neat collection of French-based producers – and a short menu of relaxed, homey dishes. Breakfast is a treat; try the *shakshuka* (baked eggs) served with feta, or toasted banana bread, which is smeared with a salted butter.
3 rue Neuve Popincourt, 11e,
www.cafeoberkampf.com

Stern Caffè

This Italian all-dayer in the 19th-century retail arcade passage des Panoramas is owned by the Alajmo family, famed for the revered restaurant Le Calandre in Padua, Italy, and features interiors by Philippe Starck. As is his wont, the designer has deployed stuffed coyotes, an ex-rabbit, hats as lampshades, and a wall of curios, and somehow it actually gels with the Cordoba leather walls and parquet floors of this former stationery shop (note the sign outside). The offering is excellent, from the first espresso of the day, served in golden Stern coffee cups, to Campari spritz and *cicchetti* for the *apéro* before cep risotto with white truffles and cream, or seabass carpaccio with caviar. There's an extensive list of sparkling whites.
47 passage des Panoramas, 2ᵉ,
T 75 43 63 10, www.caffestern.com

Café Kitsuné

Le Palais-Royal is a narrow slice of prime fashion real estate – Acne, Rick Owens and Stella McCartney moved in to its 17th-century colonnades a few years ago. Café Kitsuné is perfect for a retail pitstop, fun and frothy and popular with the cool kids, much like the French/Japanese record label and streetwear brand it sprang from. Coffee is brewed from sustainable Daterra beans from Brazil. Order with a fox-shaped biscuit (*kitsune* is Japanese for 'fox') or a slice of gluten-free cake. On hotter days, try the iced *matcha* (green tea). Kitsuné merchandise (bags and caps) is on sale; sadly, the Jean-Philippe Delhomme fox painting is not. The parquet, mouldings and signage are relics from the premises' former incarnation as a textile workshop.
51 galerie de Montpensier, 1er,
T 40 15 62 31, www.kitsune.fr

Les Bains Bar
An infamous late-night haunt of the
glitterati in the 1980s and 1990s, Les
Bains was reborn as a boutique hotel
in 2015. The bar, conceived by architect
Vincent Bastie, drips with red lacquer,
and features original tiling designed by
Philippe Starck in 1978. The cocktails
are served with flair; try a Popolo Rosso,
a mix of Monkey 47 gin and blood orange.
7 rue du Bourg-l'Abbé, 3ᵉ, T 42 77 07 07

La Buvette

This miniscule wine bar, with its broken tile flooring, 1930s oak counter and just a couple of tables, represents much that is current in Parisian gastronomy. Camille Fourmont, previously at the refined tapas and wine bar Le Dauphin (T 55 28 78 88), operates in a lo-fi, sort of old-fashioned style, although her choice of alimentation is anything but, offering elite products at non-scary prices. There is no kitchen as such, just a dinky prep area; listed on the blackboard (actually a mirror) are small plates, perhaps duck magret with Bordier raspberry butter, or Trikalinos sardines with yuzu vinegar. Wine comes courtesy of Laurent Saillard in the Loire and Nicolas Vauthier in Avallon, while the beer hails from the local Goutte d'Or brewery. Look out for the neon sign.
67 rue Saint-Maur, 11ᵉ, T 09 83 56 94 11

Le Mary Celeste

There is much that is welcoming about Le Mary Celeste, and the patient staff will find you a perch when it's busy (it's always busy) and chat even when the pressure's on. It occupies a premium position on a street corner, and has expansive windows and a sociable hexagonal bar centre stage. Kick into evening mode with a potent cocktail, such as the Don Cenobio, made with Arette tequila, Merlet crème de poire, white port, lemon juice and agave syrup, or a glass of Jacques Selosse fizz. Mads Christensen's inventive menu changes weekly, usually featuring oysters in season, and perhaps lamb tacos with pickled aubergine. The owners also run nearby Candelaria (T 42 74 41 28) and Glass (T 09 80 72 98 83) in the 9th, both beloved of the party crowd.
1 rue Commines, 3ᵉ, T 09 80 72 98 83, www.lemaryceleste.com

Clamato

Fans of Septime (see p052) are all aglow about this next-door offshoot, which has a looser, later vibe, a no-reservations policy, and a globetrotting, ocean-going menu quite unlike more traditional Paris seafood joints. The cabin-esque interior features parquet bricks on the floor that continue up the side of the bar, bench seating, wood tables and a pine-clad ceiling. Arrive when the doors open at 7pm, or after 9.30pm,

to avoid the crowds, and order to share. Start with clams – ask your server for the *plus fines* – and *pouce-pied* (gooseneck barnacles) with marigold vinaigrette (very Noma), followed by grey mullet ceviche, and smoked haddock served with shiitake. The puddings are fantastic too, notably the maple syrup tart with Chantilly cream. *80 rue de Charonne, 11ᵉ, T 43 72 74 53, www.septime-charonne.fr*

Septime

Bertrand Grébaut has cooked at L'Arpège (T 47 05 09 06) alongside Alain Passard, a 'natural' chef who inspired Noma and the New Nordics. Now he serves brilliant *bistronomie* near Bastille in his low-key, buzzy dining room. There is a farmhouse feel thanks to the rough-plastered walls, weathered tables and oxidised mirrors, as well as an iron spiral staircase and vintage bell-jar pendant lights. Simply request either 'red' or 'white' for your aperitif, divulge any food intolerances, and the rest is decided for you. The €70 carte blanche menu makes the most of what's in season, in dishes such as cod with asparagus and grilled nasturtium leaves or duck with yellow beetroot. The modish desserts avoid pastry and cream. *80 rue de Charonne, 11ᵉ, T 43 67 38 29, www.septime-charonne.fr*

Saturne

Chef Sven Chartier, just 24 years old at the
time, opened Saturne with the sommelier
Ewen Lemoigne in 2010. The pared-back,
Scandi-style interior features undressed
tables, Jean Louis Iratzoki's felt- and wool-
covered oak 'Laia' chairs, stone walls and
an open kitchen, illuminated by a giant
skylight and light fittings by Serge Mouille
and Céline Wright. The €45 lunch menu
and €75 'surprise' dinner of six courses
deploy impeccably sourced ingredients
in dishes such as smoked beef tartare
with fermented anchovies, and grilled
wild turbot with bergamot, clams and
red sorrel. *Vins naturels* from the Loire,
Auvergne, Languedoc and Savoie are
ambrosial, particularly with Lemoigne's
guidance. Saturne is closed at weekends.
*17 rue Notre-Dame des Victoires, 2ᵉ,
T 42 60 31 90, www.saturne-paris.fr*

INSIDERS' GUIDE

CHARLOTTE DE TONNAC AND HUGO SAUZAY, DESIGNERS

Charlotte de Tonnac and Hugo Sauzay of Festen Architecture live and work out of their Haussmannian-style Haut-Marais flat, a spot they enjoy for its Parisian authenticity and central location. It's also within walking distance of some of their favourite stores, like Ofr bookshop (see p080), where they pick up photography titles and rare editions, and menswear boutique Éditions MR (10 boulevard des Filles du Calvaire, 11e, T 48 04 06 08): 'The coats are perfectly cut in a classic French style,' says Sauzay. They will often stroll to Bob's Kitchen (74 rue de Gravilliers, 3e, T 52 55 11 66) for a simple lunch, perhaps brown rice with roasted vegetables, lemon confit and basil. When they have the time, they rise early and visit the main courtyard at the Louvre (see p029), best seen at first light. They also like Le Bal (6 impasse de la Défense, 18e, T 44 70 75 50), for contemporary visual art, Jakob + Macfarlane's pea-green Cité de la Mode et du Design (34 quai d'Austerlitz, 13e, T 76 77 25 30) and Musée National Gustave Moreau (14 rue de La Rochefoucauld, 9e, T 48 74 38 50), set in the Symbolist painter's apartment and studio.

They often dine at Japanese bistro SŌMA (see p032), where the beef tataki and miso spinach ticks the boxes, followed by drinks at La Buvette (see p048). If late-night dancing is on the cards, they head to the happening hotel bar at Le Pigalle (see p022), and order a Kir du Pigalle, made with crème de cassis, white wine and Salers. *For full addresses, see Resources.*

ART AND DESIGN
GALLERIES, STUDIOS AND PUBLIC SPACES

The art scene in Paris has always leaned towards the highbrow, and it is perhaps becoming more so as it internationalises, with dealers such as Galerie Kreo (31 rue Dauphine, 6e, T 53 10 23 00) and Carpenters Workshop Gallery (54 rue de la Verrerie, 4e, T 42 78 80 92) maintaining premises both here and in London.

Midcentury French design remains as significant and covetable as ever, with Patrick Seguin (see p069) and Pascal Cuisinier (13 rue de Seine, 6e, T 43 54 34 61) devoting essential shows to stellar makers. In terms of the contemporary, it's worth seeking out fresh spaces making waves on the city's fringes, such as Until Then (see p058) and Galerie Allen (see p063). And the line between furniture and art has become more blurred than ever at Gosserez (3 rue Debelleyme, 3e, T 06 12 29 90 40), S Bensimon (111 rue de Turenne, 3e, T 42 74 50 77) and Galerie BSL (23 rue Charlot, 3e, T 44 78 94 14), where Noé Duchaufour-Lawrance's sinuous Corian wave has been employed as a display device. All these three are clustered in the Haut-Marais, offering a snapshot of a refreshing hybrid creativity.

Fondation Louis Vuitton (see p060) is the most talked-about public arrival, along with the reopened Musée Picasso (5 rue de Thorigny, 3e, T 85 56 00 36), which took double the time and euros to restore than expected, and now has 37 galleries. Out of town, the modern collides with history at the Palace of Versailles (see p068). *For full addresses, see Resources.*

Robert Stadler

Vienna-born, Paris-based designer Robert Stadler's practice merges craftsmanship with cutting-edge technology. The precise, slender 2015 'Pow' table is a case in point; it is constructed from black carbon fibre legs with an iridescent glass top that shifts hues depending on your perspective. His concept-driven furniture melds elegance and gaucheness, precious and lo-fi, and is as tactile as it is visual. The pleated 'Pli Bleu' shelf (above) was commissioned by Kvadrat in 2014 and is crafted from its felt-like 'Divina' fabric to mark the 30th anniversary of the textile; when mounted flat against a wall, its central fold functions as a ledge for displaying small objects. Find Stadler's pieces at Carpenters Workshop (opposite) and Triple V (T 45 84 08 36), well worth a trip for its avant-garde roster. *www.robertstadler.net*

Until Then

Olivier Belot, Mélanie Meffrer Rondeau and Alexa Brossard, alumni from the now shuttered Yvon Lambert, have positioned themselves outside the anachronistic art world of the well-heeled Marais, or boho Belleville, and headed north, setting up shop adjacent to the Marché aux Puces de Saint-Ouen at Clignancourt. The site itself represents a break from the usual white-cube mould, and is an informal 500 sq m hangar-like space. Since opening in 2015, Until Then has exhibited work by blue-chip artists, such as Douglas Gordon, Joan Jonas and the legendary Robert Barry, as well as that by emerging names like Alin Bozbiciu, who displayed intimate oil paintings in his 2016 show 'After the Sacrifice' (above), and young Chinese talent Zhuo Qi (opposite).
77 rue des Rosiers, T 85 58 40 22,
www.untilthen.fr

Fondation Louis Vuitton

Frank Gehry's peacocking glass sails envelop 3,850 sq m of exhibition space, much of it sparsely populated, for LV billionaire Bernard Arnault to show off his art. This contentious 2014 museum rises above the treeline in the formerly protected Bois de Boulogne. A 'gift' to the city or vanity project? Time will tell.

8 avenue du Mahatma Gandhi, 16ᵉ, T 40 69 96 00, www.fondationlouisvuitton.fr

Galerie des Galeries

Set on the first floor of department store Galeries Lafayette (T 42 82 34 56), this low-ceilinged, unusually shaped room provides the setting for four shows a year that meld fashionable presentations with curatorial clout. The French artist Xavier Veilhan's 'On/Off', for example, was a multisensory exploration into the crossover between contemporary art and music, and LA-based photographer Alex Prager held her first solo outing in the country here. The group exhibition 'All Over' (above), curated by Samuel Gross, pulled together a dizzying spectacle of work based on vertical stripes by mainly Swiss creatives, as well as former YBA painter Ian Davenport and Italian op artist Domenico Battista, whose canvases of contrasting lines generate moiré waves. *40 boulevard Haussmann, 9ᵉ, T 42 82 81 98, www.galeriedesgaleries.com*

Galerie Allen

Despite its relatively modest size and lo-fi fit-out, featuring simple parquetry floors and strip lighting, Galerie Allen has made quite a splash within the Paris art scene. Helmed by two Australian expats – artist Mel O'Callaghan and curator Joseph Allen Shea – it represents a small but influential stable of talent, including photo and video artist Colin Snapp, and the estate of Corita Kent. A somewhat unsung hero of the pop art movement here, Kent's work had little visibility in France until now; the Centre Pompidou (see p010) has since acquired pieces from the gallery. In 2015, Linus Bill + Adrien Horni showed a series of abstract paintings ('Gemälde', above) exploring the effect of duplication, deconstruction and reappropriation on an image's integrity. *59 rue de Dunkerque, 9e, T 45 26 92 33, www.galerieallen.com*

Vallois

Championing the New Realists, as well as emerging talent, this gallery has racked up a quarter of a century in Saint-Germain-des-Prés. It represents Jacques Villeglé, famed for his Lettrist and poster art from the 1950s on; sculptor and painter Niki de Saint Phalle; and Swiss Dadaist Jean Tinguely. Contemporary artists who have been granted solo shows are Americans Paul McCarthy and Jeff Mills, erstwhile YBA Keith Tyson, and French counterparts Alain Bublex and Gilles Barbier. There is also a fine publishing arm – Vallois' 2012 monograph on Tinguely includes pieces unseen for 50 years. The gallery recently took on the estate of pop art painter Alain Jacquet, while Virginie Yassef's 'Au Milieu du Crétacé' (above) was a past highlight. *36 rue de Seine, 6ᵉ, T 46 34 61 07, www.galerie-vallois.com*

Galerie Thaddaeus Ropac

Established in 2012, this is the Austrian gallerist Thaddaeus Ropac's second Paris-based venture – his first is in the Marais (T 42 72 99 00). The huge site is situated in the working-class suburb of Pantin, just beyond the Périphérique. Formerly a 20th-century ironworks factory, it was overhauled by architects Buttazzoni & Associés, and the red-brick structure now houses 2,500 sq m of exhibition space within four halls – it's the perfect canvas for large-scale shows by the likes of heavyweights Gilbert & George, Tony Cragg, Alex Katz and Anselm Kiefer ('Die Ungeborenen', above). The gallery is a half-hour trip from the centre on the Métro; combine your visit with a stop at the Philharmonie de Paris (see p074). *69 avenue du Général Leclerc, Pantin, T 55 89 01 10, www.ropac.net*

Wonmin Park

Seoul-born, Paris-based Wonmin Park – a Design Academy Eindhoven graduate who has exhibited at Musée des Arts Décoratifs (T 44 55 57 50) – is perhaps best known for his dreamy resin furniture collection. 'Haze Armchair' (above) is a 2015 addition to the series, which also includes a stool and a table, cast in a palette of muted red, yellow and green. The project is imbued with an intriguing tension: the translucent, minimal slabs are seemingly ethereal, but as a complete work create functional forms. The project is developed at the Carpenters Workshop Gallery research centre, which is set in a former varnish factory in Roissy. Purchase works from its showroom in the Marais (see p056), or visit Park's studio by appointment. *13-15 rue Fernand Forest, Mitry-Mory, www.wonminpark.com*

Lustre Gabriel, Versailles

The monumental staircase leading to the Grands Apartments at Versailles was designed in 1772 by Louis XV's architect Ange-Jacques Gabriel, but construction came to a halt – for 200 years. Now the neoclassical austerity has been leavened by Ronan and Erwan Bouroullec's *Lustre Gabriel* chandelier: a 12m-high luminous artwork formed of three organic-looking loops of crystal and LED. The brothers from Breton worked alongside technicians at Swarovski to engineer the discreet joints and cables that allow the 800 glowing links to hang so elegantly. Versailles' protectors are said to have only given permission for the installation of a contemporary artwork in the Ancien Régime reliquary because the staircase itself is effectively new.
Palace of Versailles, T 30 83 78 00, www.chateauversailles.fr

Galerie Patrick Seguin

This voluminous furniture repository is owned by Patrick and Laurence Seguin. Behind a rather deceptive facade (above), remodelled in 2013, is Jean Nouvel's deft conversion of an old carpentry workshop, which has been painted white, its beams exposed, and flooded with light through a glass roof. On show are decorative pieces and furnishings by the most eminent midcentury architects and designers in France – legends including Jean Prouvé, Charlotte Perriand, Pierre Jeanneret and Le Corbusier (all of whom are represented overleaf). Its publishing initiative produces definitive monographs on Prouvé, and a few others. Seguin curates exhibitions at institutions such as New York's MoMA and the Vitra Design Museum in Weil am Rhein. *5 rue des Taillandiers, 11ᵉ, T 47 00 32 35, www.patrickseguin.com*

ARCHITOUR

A GUIDE TO THE CITY'S ICONIC BUILDINGS

There are a dozen Le Corbusier buildings in and around Paris, the city in which he lived and worked for most of his adult life. Today, some, such as Villa Besnus (85 boulevard de la République), the family home he completed in 1922 in the suburb of Vaucresson, are almost unrecognisable. Others, such as the 1951 Maisons Jaoul (81 rue de Longchamp) in verdant Neuilly-sur-Seine, which were gossip-magazine staples when they belonged to Lord Palumbo and served as a base for his friends (including Diana, Princess of Wales), have been carefully restored. Most of Le Corbusier's Paris projects are concentrated in a crescent across the southern half of the city and can be squeezed into half a day's architourism, or combined, as we suggest, with a selection of other modern gems.

Cité de Refuge (12 rue Cantagrel, 13ᵉ) is a good start. Nearby is Maison Planeix (24 bis boulevard Masséna, 13ᵉ). A house/studio, it was designed for one of Corbu's most ardent, if impecunious, clients, the sculptor Antonin Planeix. Atelier Ozenfant (53 avenue Reille, 14ᵉ) is another of the architect's live/work spaces. By the early 1930s, Le Corbusier was back in the 14th for his first public commission, Pavillon Suisse. He revisited the site for Maison du Brésil (7 boulevard Jourdan, 14ᵉ, T 58 10 23 00) in 1959. Fondation Le Corbusier can advise (by phone or email) on itineraries, which should include the neighbouring Maison La Roche (opposite).
For full addresses, see Resources.

Maison La Roche

One of the early benchmarks of modern architecture, the 1923 Maison La Roche and adjoining 1925 Maison Jeanneret (home to the Fondation Le Corbusier) – are worth a detour to the sleepy 16th. It was designed primarily to house the art collection of Swiss banker Raoul La Roche in a central gallery (above) and offers an insight into Le Corbusier's experiments with private versus public space, showcasing his use of polychromatic colour – burnt orange, sky blue, dusty pink – to play with volumes. He installed an interior ramp, which he called a 'promenade', to orchestrate a series of shifting viewpoints. Restored in 2009, the property features Corbu furniture, such as built-in storage units, Thonet chairs, Berber rugs and rotating artworks in situ.
10 square du Docteur Blanche, 16e,
T 42 88 41 53, www.fondationlecorbusier.fr

Philharmonie de Paris

Soaring costs, cut corners and a premature opening (two years late) led to Jean Nouvel denouncing his project, yet we rather like it. The bent, folded planes of the concert hall are clad in an aluminium and steel mesh, whose nuances, from silver to charcoal, glisten in the sun and evoke a flock of birds. The voluptuous balconies and ramps of the 2,400-seat auditorium are impressive too.

221 avenue Jean Jaurès, 19ᵉ

Fondation Jérôme Seydoux-Pathé

Renzo Piano's organic bulge in the Paris cityscape colonises the courtyard of a Haussmann-era block near place d'Italie, an 'unexpected presence' connected to the 19th-century buildings at four points. Only a sliver of its five storeys is glimpsed over the roofline. This HQ for the Jérôme Seydoux-Pathé film foundation contains exhibition space, a 68-seater screening room, archives and offices. Entrance is via the listed 1869 facade, beautifully sculpted by Rodin, and a skylit atrium. From here, bridges lead into the curvaceous carapace of glass tiles, underpinned by timber ribs, that allows soft light into the upper levels, which are linked by a spiral staircase. Open 1pm to 6pm, Tuesday to Friday; 10am to 7pm, Saturday (€6 entry includes a film). *73 avenue des Gobelins, 13ᵉ, T 83 79 18 96, www.fondation-jeromeseydoux-pathe.com*

Maison de Verre

One of the greatest houses built in the International Style is one of the least visited. Architects Pierre Chareau and Bernard Bijvoet, together with metal craftsman Louis Dalbet, worked wonders on the bones of an existing building on a small plot in the 7th arrondissement, completing the new structure in 1932. The facades are covered with glass blocks set into a steel frame, which creates a well of light while also ensuring privacy. The living room is the real show-stopper. It features steel columns with exposed bolts and thin slabs of slate, and a sliding-panel bookcase that covers one wall. Wires were threaded through metal tubing that runs from floor to ceiling. It is only open to architects, who must apply for a tour in writing; there is a six-month waiting list.
31 rue Saint-Guillaume, 7ᵉ

Communist Party Headquarters

The French Communist Party is blessed with a superlative seat from which to orchestrate its policies. Designed by architect Oscar Niemeyer (a committed communist), its HQ is one of the city's finest pieces of modernist architecture: an undulating glazed building with a series of subterranean chambers. The highlight is the sculptural conference hall, which has a white domed roof that rises in front of the primary structure. Niemeyer collaborated with Jean Prouvé on the sinuous glass curtain wall and its mechanical window openers, and designed the furniture. Free tours can be arranged by appointment, or you may be invited to an event – Prada and Dior have rented the building for shows.
2 place du Colonel Fabien, 19ᵉ,
T 40 40 12 12

SHOPS

THE BEST RETAIL THERAPY AND WHAT TO BUY

At the fashion and beauty houses, radical architecture and design is vital. In 2010, <u>Balenciaga</u> (10 avenue George V, 8e, T 47 20 21 11) unveiled a spacecraft-like flagship devised by Nicolas Ghesquière and artist Dominique Gonzalez-Foerster. For its store on the Rive Gauche, <u>Hermès</u> (17 rue de Sèvres, 6e, T 42 22 80 83) built some striking installations made from woven ash; furniture design is integral to <u>Balmain</u> (see p088) and <u>Alaïa</u> (see p092); and art, not bling, defines <u>Guerlain</u>'s rebirth (see p094). For a more homespun affair, gents are catered for at knitwear label <u>Monsieur Lacenaire</u> (57 rue Charlot, 3e, T 42 77 36 04) and <u>Ami</u> (22 rue de Grenelle, 7e, T 09 82 30 96 77), where the menswear designed by Alexandre Mattiussi is hip (pattern, oversize) and dandy (linen, toile).

The Colette effect is still in evidence, notably at concept stores <u>Centre Commercial</u> (2 rue de Marseille, 10e, T 42 02 26 08) and <u>Merci</u> (111 boulevard Beaumarchais, 3e, T 42 77 00 33), housed in an 1840 former wallpaper factory. Here you could find a jacket by Rains, a Paola Navone sofa and Cutipol cutlery, with profits going to charity. Also check out <u>Chez Moi</u> (25 rue Hérold, 1er, T 06 61 26 23 31), which is presented as a living space. And this being Paris, there is an erudite theme to the retail landscape, especially in the highly browsable <u>Ofr</u> (20 rue Dupetit-Thouars, 3e, T 42 45 72 88) and <u>LO/A</u> (17 rue Notre Dame de Nazareth, 3e, T 09 83 75 91 08). *For full addresses, see Resources.*

Paco Rabanne

This is the first Paco Rabanne store to open in 14 years, and is testament to the contemporary vision that artistic director Julien Dossena has for the heritage brand. He collaborated with Belgian architects Kersten Geers and David Van Severen on the interiors, which are modelled on a toolbox. Perforated aluminium panelling and cabinets, for instance, are functional and also pure Paco Rabanne; edgy and utilitarian, part throwback yet thoroughly modern. Chrome fixtures are contrasted with blush-hued leather floor tiles across two compact, refined spaces. Ready-to-wear is displayed in the main area (above) and a corridor houses accessories – look out for the iconic chain mail. The ambient scent is by perfumer Dominique Ropion. *12 rue Cambon, 1er, T 42 36 22 26, www.pacorabanne.com*

Études

The flagship store for Études Studio, which produces a hip line in menswear and artist books from offices in Paris and New York, was designed by local firm Ciguë. Situated off a small courtyard, it is slender, polished and minimal, given colour through artworks by seasonal collaborators like Linus Bill + Adrien Horni (see p063). We took home a wool felt hat in the label's signature blue.
14 rue Debelleyme, 3e, T 49 96 56 62

Le Baigneur

Established in 2012 by Fabien Meaudre, Le Baigneur (The Bather) creates face and body products for gents from organic and natural ingredients. Bol et Savon à Barbe No 2 (above), for instance, is made from St John's Wort, oat extracts, honey, lavender and purifying yellow clay, and comes in a neat porcelain vessel by Artoria Limoges; we also like the Huile de Prune Noisette, a luxe oil crafted from cold-pressed plum pips grown in Lot-et-Garonne. The brand offers shaving accoutrements too, such as a beech-handled brush with badger hair bristles that is assembled in Brittany. The handsome tri-tone packaging, designed by local firm Atelier Müesli, is entirely recyclable. You can find items at Galeries Lafayette (see p062) and accessories store Ateliers Auguste (T 48 05 91 36). *www.lebaigneur.fr*

Officine Universelle Buly

You don't walk out of this store with only a Retour d'Egypte candle. Perfume matches are de rigueur, naturally, but then there are the clays for home facials, vegetable oils (certainly not the cooking kind) and, if you're not body brushing with a horsehair glove, well... Buly's products are paraben-free, and the fragrances are formulated without the use of alcohol to make them subtle and true – try the Lichen d'Ecosse,

Rose de Damas or Bergamote. Defer to the knowledgeable staff, purchase the house Pommade Virginale ointment, sing along to the opera and depart happy. The gorgeous interior – a reimagining of a historic Buly *officine* inhabiting rue Montorgueil during the 19th century – is lined with wooden cabinetry and white and turquoise tiling.
6 rue Bonaparte, 6ᵉ, T 43 29 02 50, www.buly1803.com

Rue Hérold
This light-filled fabric shop is owned by Charlotte de La Grandière, who favours natural fibres, like fine Belgian linens, and Italian cottons and wools, mainly in neutral tones and sun-washed colours. They are sold by the metre, or you can commission bespoke soft furnishings. Find her modish textiles, such as velvet curtains, at red-hot Le Pigalle (see p022). *8 rue Hérold, 1er, T 42 33 66 56*

Balmain

The achingly elegant and graceful flagship of this Parisian fashion house whispers chic, as you might expect from Balmain. Housed in Pierre Balmain's former studio, founded in 1945, the first-floor boutique underwent a 21st-century makeover, and relaunched in 2010. The architect, Joseph Dirand, given free rein by the label's then creative director, Christophe Decarnin, restored the original cornicing, marble fireplaces and the untreated Versailles parquet flooring to create a showroom *ne plus ultra*, in which the decor demands as much attention as the fashion. Decarnin accented the space with furniture of his own design, a console by Gilbert Poillerat, master of wrought iron, and a table by the late sculptor André Arbus.

44 rue François 1er, 8ᵉ, T 47 20 35 34, www.balmain.com

Nose

Nicolas Cloutier and Mark Buxton are key members of the seven-strong team that launched Nose, a 'diagnostic' perfumery offering more than a spritz of the latest couture fragrance. Instead, customers are gently quizzed about their olfactory whims and wishes before being guided towards a handful of potions that might suit. Apart from expertise and a certain sense of ceremony, what's on offer is an ahead-of-the-curve selection of scents, from Brooklyn-based DS & Durga and Dr Vranjes to Miller et Bertaux and Comme Des Garçons. The 175 sq m shop, replete with fridge-style storage, also stocks beauty products by Retrouvé and Joëlle Ciocco, and treats for the home by Astier de Villatte, Malin + Goetz and Cire Trudon. *20 rue Bachaumont, 2ᵉ, T 40 26 46 03, www.nose.fr*

L/Uniform

The meticulous fit-out here, by architect Masamichi Katayama, who also designed cult concept store Colette (T 55 35 33 90), is compartmentalised in a manner that befits the uber-utilitarian, refined canvas bags on display. To simplify the selection process, each style – from backpacks to satchels, totes and pouches, all of which are crafted in Carcassonne – is named, numbered and allocated its own console.

A replica workshop at the back of the store (opposite), clad in oak parquet, provides inspiration for customisation: the weave, be it army-style short-card cotton or water-resistant linen, as well as the trim, can be ordered bespoke, and initials silk-screened onto any model, like the covetable Carry-on Suitcase No 40 (above), from €1,400.
21 quai Malaquais, 6e, T 42 61 76 27, www.luniform.com

Boutique Alaïa

Living legend Azzedine Alaïa called on his
friends Marc Newson and Kris Ruhs to help
him create this unforgettable space in a
three-storey 18th-century *hôtel particulier*.
Newson contributed the impressive circular
light fixtures that embellish each floor, and
Ruhs designed a sculptural brushed-steel
chandelier for the marble staircase. Pierre
Paulin pieces appear throughout, as well
as two Charlotte Perriand tables and, in the
courtyard (opposite), where you can take
tea, Harry Bertoia chairs. The green wall
here is by the botanist Patrick Blanc, who
pioneered the trend in Paris. Accessories
are on the ground floor, and clothing is
upstairs, on Martin Szekely-designed racks.
The paintings by Alaïa's partner, Christoph
Von Weyhe, are of the Hamburg docks.
*5 rue de Marignan, 8ᵉ, T 76 72 91 11,
www.alaia.fr*

L'Institut Guerlain

Peter Marino, known for his boutiques for Chanel, Dior and Fendi, led the renovation of Guerlain's Champs-Élysées HQ, which was designed in 1914 by Charles Mewès, architect of the Ritz. The 1828 brand has been enshrined here in straw marquetry, a crystal-studded Proust quote, Calacatta marble, hefty Baccarat chandeliers and an installation of inflatable golden bees. In the extension dedicated to make-up, beauty and edible delicacies, the 19,873 glassy eyes of a Norbert Brunner artwork follow you around as you browse. A white bronze orchid by Marc Quinn decorates the mezzanine, past which any VIP clients are ushered to inhale rarities. On the first floor, listed Jean-Michel Frank interiors and cut onyx are deployed to heady effect (opposite). There is also an on-site spa.
68 avenue des Champs-Élysées, 8ᵉ,
T 45 62 11 21, www.guerlain.com

ESCAPES

WHERE TO GO IF YOU WANT TO LEAVE TOWN

When they periodically abandon their city, where do Parisians go? The fact is, it's nowhere near Paris. If it's not Punta del Este or Sicily, it'll be sunny Île de Ré off La Rochelle, the leafy Limousin, or good old Provence. You ought to take advantage of the expanded TGV network, to make it to Le Havre in two hours for an Auguste Perret architour, nip to Deauville for the seafood and beaches, or make a gastro pilgrimage to La Grenouillère (19 rue de la Grenouillère, T 03 21 06 07 22), about an hour's journey from Gare du Nord via Arras. A scant two-and-a-half hours west, France's sixth-largest city, Nantes, has an outpost of the contemporary Galerie Melanie Rio (34 boulevard Guist'hau, T 02 40 89 20 40); stay at Okko (15 rue de Strasbourg, T 02 52 20 00 70), which has a luxe feel minus the spend. If you're heading south, take your leave by lingering over *un allongé* amid the overblown rococo of Le Train Bleu dining room at the Gare de Lyon (1st floor, place Louis Armand, 12e, T 43 43 09 06).

Closer to home, the MAC/VAL museum (place de la Libération, T 43 91 64 20), set in parkland in the south-eastern suburb of Vitry-sur-Seine, is a pleasant half-day diversion, or lose an afternoon in Le Pré Catelan restaurant (route de la Grande Cascade, 16e, T 44 14 41 14) in the Bois de Boulogne. Le Corbusier's 1931 Villa Savoye (82 rue de Villiers, T 39 65 01 06) is in Poissy, to the north-west. This 'box in the air' is the purest of his purist villas – don't miss it. *For full addresses, see Resources.*

Fontevraud L'Hôtel, Loire Valley

This ultra-pared-back hotel and fine-diner is set inside a 12th-century abbey complex close to the picturesque town of Saumur, a three-and-a-half-hour drive from Paris. The Saint-Lazare priory was overhauled by designers Patrick Jouin and Sanjit Manku, who retained the chalky limestone walls and arched ceilings in the iBar (above) and introduced screens made from a stretch-knit fabric by Innofa to soften acoustics.

The accommodation is similarly monastic, featuring custom-made oak furniture and natural-hued linens. Young chef Thibaut Ruggeri helms the on-site restaurant, and turns out creative dishes using seasonal, locally sourced produce – including herbs grown in the kitchen garden – served on stoneware by the ceramicist Charles Hair.
38 rue Saint-Jean de l'Habit,
Fontevraud-l'Abbaye, T 02 46 46 10 10

Louvre-Lens

The selection in 2004 of industrial Lens, two hours north of the capital between Amiens and Lille, as host for an extension of one of the world's elite museums (the shortlist included Boulogne-sur-Mer and Calais) screamed cultural democratisation. No mere satellite of its progenitor, Louvre-Lens, opened in 2012, has been conceived to bring art to the people via multimedia tools and attendants more likely to engage you in conversation than lay down the law. Exhibits in the Glass Pavilion synchronise with regional galleries across France; the 3,000 sq m Grande Galerie shows works from the Louvre's collection. SANAA's low steel-and-glass structures let in light and reflect the surrounding landscaped park, which was built on a defunct coal mine. *99 rue Paul Bert, Lens, T 03 21 18 62 62, www.louvrelens.fr*

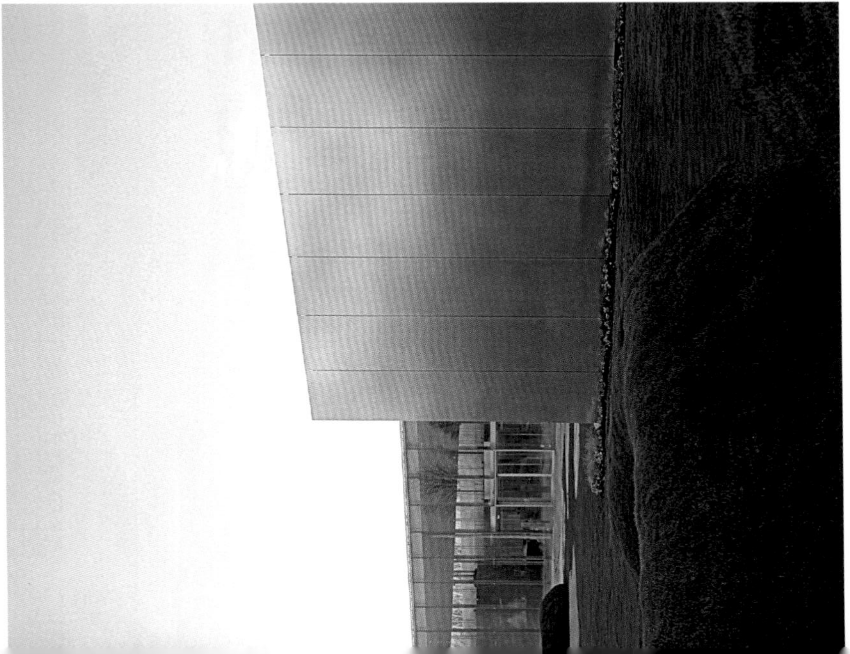

Créteil Cathédrale, Créteil

The ambitious expansion of the cathedral of Notre Dame de Créteil, designed by Charles-Gustave Stoskopf in 1978, was led by the Paris firm Architecture-Studio and finished in 2015. A pair of wood-clad hulls form a soaring domed roof, which rises out of the original white concrete structure and evokes two hands clasped in prayer (above). At the juncture, a strip of stained glass by artists Udo Zembok and Pascale Zembok allows for gentle tinted light to permeate the liturgical space. The sparse interiors are clad with parallel rib-like Douglas fir beams that stretch up to 22m high. Minimal benches are arranged in a semicircle around the altar. There's also a café and bookshop on site, which is a 45-minute train ride south-west from Paris. *2 rue André Maurois, T 45 17 24 00, www.creteilcathedrale.fr*

Le Château, Rentilly
In the eastern suburbs, this 16th-century château (wrecked in WWII) was reborn in 2014 as a contemporary art space, by artist Xavier Veilhan, set designer Alexis Bertrand and architects Bona-Lemercier, who cloaked the entire facade in mirror-polished stainless steel. It produces a clever camouflage effect on sunny days. *Parc Culturel de Rentilly, 1 rue de l'Étang, Bussy-Saint-Martin, T 60 35 46 72*

NOTES
SKETCHES AND MEMOS

RESOURCES

CITY GUIDE DIRECTORY

A

Ami 080
22 rue de Grenelle, 7^e
T 09 82 30 96 77
www.amiparis.fr

L'Arpège 052
84 rue de Varenne, 7^e
T 47 05 09 06
www.alain-passard.com

Les Arpenteurs 023
9 rue Choron, 9^e
T 53 16 47 96

L'Astrance 032
4 rue Beethoven, 16^e
T 40 50 84 40
www.astrancerestaurant.com

Atelier Ozenfant 072
53 avenue Reille, 14^e
www.fondationlecorbusier.fr

Ateliers Auguste 084
8 rue de Turenne, 4^e
T 48 05 91 36
www.ateliers-auguste.fr

Aux Deux Amis 024
45 rue Oberkampf, 11^e
T 58 30 38 13

B

Le Baigneur 084
www.lebaigneur.fr

Les Bains Bar 046
7 rue du Bourg-l'Abbé, 3^e
T 42 77 07 07
www.lesbains-paris.com

Le Bal 054
6 impasse de la Défense, 18^e
T 44 70 75 50
www.le-bal.fr

Le Bal Café 024
6 impasse de la Défense, 18^e
T 44 70 75 51
www.le-bal.fr

Balenciaga 080
10 avenue George V, 8^e
T 47 20 21 11
www.balenciaga.com

Balmain 088
44 rue François 1er, 8^e
T 47 20 35 34
www.balmain.com

Bob's Kitchen 054
74 rue de Gravilliers, 3^e
T 52 55 11 66
www.bobsjuicebar.com

Boot Café 043
19 rue du Pont aux Choux, 3^e
T 73 70 14 57
www.cargocollective.com/bootcafe

Boutique Alaïa 092
5 rue de Marignan, 8^e
T 76 72 91 11
www.alaia.fr

Boutique Yam'Tcha 041
4 rue Sauval, 1er
T 40 26 06 06
www.yamtcha.com

Brasserie Thoumieux 039
79 rue Saint-Dominique, 7^e
T 47 05 79 00
www.thoumieux.fr

The Broken Arm 025
12 rue Perrée, 3^e
T 44 61 53 60
www.the-broken-arm.com

La Buvette 048
67 rue Saint-Maur, 11^e
T 09 83 56 94 11

C

Café Kitsuné 045
  51 galerie de Montpensier, 1er
  T 40 15 62 31
  www.kitsune.fr

Café Oberkampf 043
  3 rue Neuve Popincourt, 11e
  www.cafeoberkampf.com

Caillebotte 042
  8 rue Hippolyte Lebas, 9e
  T 53 20 88 70

Candelaria 049
  52 rue de Saintonge, 3e
  T 42 74 41 28
  www.candelariaparis.com

Carpenters Workshop Gallery 056
  54 rue de la Verrerie, 4e
  T 42 78 80 92
  www.carpentersworkshopgallery.com

Centre Commercial 080
  2 rue de Marseille, 10e
  T 42 02 26 08
  www.centrecommercial.cc

Centre Pompidou 010
  Place Georges Pompidou, 4e
  T 44 78 12 33
  www.centrepompidou.fr

Centre Pompidou-Metz 011
  1 parvis des Droits-de-l'Homme
  Metz
  T 03 87 15 39 39
  www.centrepompidou-metz.fr

Le Château 102
  Parc culturelle de Rentilly
  1 rue de l'Étang
  Bussy-Saint-Martin
  Rentilly
  T 60 35 46 72
  www.fraciledefrance.com

Le Châteaubriand 032
  129 avenue Parmentier, 11e
  T 43 57 45 95
  www.lechateaubriand.net

Chez Moi 080
  25 rue Hérold, 1er
  T 06 61 26 23 31
  chezmoiparis.com

Ciel de Paris 012
  56th floor
  Tour Montparnasse
  33 avenue du Maine, 15e
  T 40 64 77 64
  www.cieldeparis.com

Cité de la Mode et du Design 054
  34 quai d'Austerlitz, 13e
  T 76 77 25 30
  www.citemodedesign.fr

Cité de Refuge 072
  12 rue Cantagrel, 13e
  www.fondationlecorbusier.fr

Clamato 050
  80 rue de Charonne, 11e
  T 43 72 74 53
  www.septime-charonne.fr

Clover 030
  5 rue Perronet, 7e
  T 75 50 00 05
  www.clover-paris.com

Clown Bar 032
  114 rue Amelot, 11e
  T 43 55 87 35

Colette 091
  213 rue Saint-Honoré, 1er
  T 55 35 33 90
  www.colette.fr

Communist Party Headquarters 078
  2 place du Colonel Fabien, 19ᵉ
  T 40 40 12 12
Cream 043
  50 rue de Belleville, 2ᵉ
  T 09 83 66 58 43
  www.cream-belleville.tumblr.com
Créteil Cathédrale 100
  2 rue André Maurois
  Créteil
  T 45 17 24 00
  www.creteilcathedrale.fr

D
Le Dauphin 048
  131 avenue Parmentier, 11ᵉ
  T 55 28 78 88
  www.restaurantledauphin.net
Department of Islamic Art 028
  Louvre
  1 place du Carrousel, 1ᵉʳ
  T 40 20 53 17
  www.louvre.fr
Dersou 036
  21 rue Saint-Nicolas, 12ᵉ
  T 09 81 01 12 73
  www.dersouparis.com
Un Dimanche à Paris 024
  4 cour du Commerce Saint-André, 6ᵉ
  T 56 81 18 18
  www.un-dimanche-a-paris.com

E
L'Ecailler du Bistrot 032
  22 rue Paul Bert, 11ᵉ
  T 43 72 76 77

Éditions MR 055
  10 boulevard des Filles du Calvaire, 11ᵉ
  T 48 04 06 08
  www.editionsmr.fr
Ellsworth 034
  34 rue de Richelieu, 1ᵉʳ
  T 42 60 59 66
  www.ellsworthparis.com
Études 082
  14 rue Debelleyme, 3ᵉ
  T 49 96 56 62
  www.etudes-studio.com

F
52 Faubourg Saint Denis 033
  52 rue du Faubourg Saint-Denis, 10ᵉ
  www.faubourgstdenis.com
Flesh 032
  25 rue de Douai, 9ᵉ
  T 42 81 21 93
  www.flesh-restaurant.com
Fondation Le Corbusier 072
  10 square du Docteur Blanche, 16ᵉ
  T 42 88 41 53
  www.fondationlecorbusier.fr
Fondation Jérôme Seydoux-Pathé 076
  73 avenue des Gobelins, 13ᵉ
  T 83 79 18 96
  www.fondation-jeromeseydoux-
  pathe.com
Fondation Louis Vuitton 060
  8 avenue du Mahatma Gandhi, 16ᵉ
  T 40 69 96 00
  www.fondationlouisvuitton.fr
Frenchie 032
  5-6 rue du Nil, 2ᵉ
  T 40 39 96 19
  www.frenchie-restaurant.com

G

Galerie Allen 063
59 rue de Dunkerque, 9e
T 45 26 92 33
www.galerieallen.com

Galerie BSL 056
23 rue Charlot, 3e
T 44 78 94 14
www.galeriebsl.com

Galerie des Galeries 062
Galeries Lafayette
40 boulevard Haussmann, 9e
T 42 82 81 98
www.galeriedesgaleries.com

Galerie Gosserez 056
3 rue Debelleyme, 3e
T 06 12 29 90 40
www.galeriegosserez.com

Galerie Kreo 056
31 rue Dauphine, 6e
T 53 10 23 00
www.galeriekreo.fr

Galerie Melanie Rio 096
34 boulevard Guist'hau
Nantes
T 02 40 89 20 40
www.rgalerie.com

Galerie Pascal Cuisinier 056
13 rue de Seine, 6e
T 43 54 34 61
www.galeriepascalcuisinier.com

Galerie Patrick Seguin 069
5 rue des Taillandiers, 11e
T 47 00 32 35
www.patrickseguin.com

Galerie Thaddaeus Ropac 066
69 avenue du Général Leclerc
Pantin
T 55 89 01 10
7 rue Debelleyme, 3e
T 42 72 99 00
www.ropac.net

Galeries Lafayette 062
40 boulevard Haussmann, 9e
T 42 82 34 56
www.galerieslafayette.com

Gallery S Bensimon 056
111 rue de Turenne, 3e
T 42 74 50 77
www.gallerybensimon.com

Gâteaux Thoumieux 039
58 rue Saint-Dominique, 7e
T 45 51 12 12
www.gateauxthoumieux.com

Glass 049
7 rue Frochot, 9e
T 09 80 72 98 83
www.glassparis.com

Le Grand Restaurant 030
7 rue d'Aguesseau, 8e
T 53 05 00 00
www.jeanfrancoispiege.com

Grande Arche de la Défense 013
1 parvis de la Défense
www.grandearche.com

Gravity Bar 031
44 rue des Vinaigriers, 10e
T 98 54 92 49

La Grenouillère 096
19 rue de la Grenouillère
La Madelaine-sous-Montreuil
T 03 21 06 07 22
www.lagrenouillere.fr

H

Hermès Sèvres 080
17 rue de Sèvres, 6ᵉ
T 42 22 80 83
www.hermes.com

I

L'Institut Guerlain 094
68 avenue des Champs-Élysées, 8ᵉ
T 45 62 11 21
www.guerlain.com

L

LiLi 020
The Peninsula
19 avenue Kléber, 16ᵉ
T 58 12 67 50
paris.peninsula.com

LO/A 080
17 rue Notre Dame de Nazareth, 3ᵉ
T 09 83 75 91 08
www.libraryofarts.com

Louvre-Lens 098
99 rue Paul Bert
Lens
T 03 21 18 62 62
www.louvrelens.fr

L/Uniform 090
21 quai Malaquais, 6ᵉ
T 42 61 76 27
www.luniform.com

Lustre Gabriel 068
Palace of Versailles
T 30 83 78 00
www.chateauversailles.fr

M

MAC/VAL 096
Place de la Libération
Vitry-sur-Seine
T 43 91 64 20
www.macval.fr

Maison du Brésil 072
71 boulevard Jourdan, 14ᵉ
T 58 10 23 00
www.maisondubresil.org

Maison Planeix 072
24 bis boulevard Masséna, 13ᵉ
www.fondationlecorbusier.fr

Maison La Roche 073
10 square du Docteur Blanche, 16ᵉ
T 42 88 41 53
www.fondationlecorbusier.fr
Closed Sundays and Monday mornings

Maison de Verre 077
31 rue Saint-Guillaume, 7ᵉ

Maisons Jaoul 072
81 rue de Longchamp
Neuilly-sur-Seine
www.fondationlecorbusier.fr

Le Mary Celeste 049
1 rue Commines, 3ᵉ
T 09 80 72 98 83
www.lemaryceleste.com

Merci 080
111 boulevard Beaumarchais, 3ᵉ
T 42 77 00 33
www.merci-merci.com

Monsieur Bleu 027
Palais de Tokyo
13 avenue du Président Wilson, 16ᵉ
T 47 20 90 47
www.monsieurbleu.com

Monsieur Lacenaire 080
57 rue Charlot, 3ᵉ
T 42 77 36 04
www.monsieurlacenaire.com
Musée des Arts Décoratifs 067
107 rue de Rivoli, 1ᵉʳ
T 44 55 57 50
www.lesartsdecoratifs.fr
Musée National Gustave Moreau 054
14 rue de La Rochefoucauld, 9ᵉ
T 48 74 38 50
www.musee-moreau.fr
Musée Picasso 056
5 rue de Thorigny, 3ᵉ
T 85 56 00 36
www.museepicassoparis.fr
Musée du quai Branly 024
37 quai Branly, 7ᵉ
T 56 61 70 00
www.quaibranly.fr

N
Night Flight 017
Hôtel Bachaumont
18 rue Bachaumont, 2ᵉ
T 48 58 56 23
www.hotelbachaumont.com
Nose 089
20 rue Bachaumont, 2ᵉ
T 40 26 46 03
www.nose.fr

O
L'Office 033
3 rue Richer, 9ᵉ
T 47 70 67 31

Officine Universelle Buly 085
6 rue Bonaparte, 6ᵉ
T 43 29 02 50
www.buly1803.com
Ofr 080
20 rue Dupetit-Thouars, 3ᵉ
T 42 45 72 88
www.ofrsystem.com
L'Oiseau Blanc 020
The Peninsula
19 avenue Kléber, 16ᵉ
T 58 12 67 30
paris.peninsula.com

P
Paco Rabanne 081
12 rue Cambon, 1ᵉʳ
T 42 36 22 26
www.pacorabanne.com
Palais de Tokyo 027
13 avenue du Président Wilson, 16ᵉ
T 81 97 35 88
www.palaisdetokyo.com
Le Pantruche 042
3 rue Victor Massé, 9ᵉ
T 48 78 55 60
Pâtisserie des Martyrs 024
22 rue des Martyrs, 9ᵉ
T 71 18 24 70
www.sebastiengaudard.com
Paul Bert 032
18 rue Paul Bert, 11ᵉ
T 43 72 24 01
Pavillon Ledoyen 032
Carré des Champs-Élysées
8 avenue Dutuit, 8ᵉ
T 53 05 10 01
www.pavillon-ledoyen.fr

Le Perchoir 024
  14 rue Crespin du Gast, 11e
  T 48 06 18 48
  www.leperchoir.fr
Philharmonie de Paris 074
  221 avenue Jean Jaurès, 19e
  www.philharmoniedeparis.fr
Le Pré Catelan 096
  Route de la Grande Cascade, 16e
  T 44 14 41 14
  www.restaurant-precatelan.com

R
Restaurant Bachaumont 017
  Hôtel Bachaumont
  18 rue Bachaumont, 2e
  T 81 66 47 50
  www.hotelbachaumont.com
Restaurant Guy Savoy 038
  Monnaie de Paris
  11 quai de Conti, 6e
  T 43 80 40 61
  www.guysavoy.com
Restaurant Yam'Tcha 040
  121 rue Saint-Honoré, 1er
  T 40 26 08 07
  www.yamtcha.com
Le Richer 033
  2 rue Richer, 9e
  www.lericher.com
Robert Stadler 057
  www.robertstadler.net
Rue Hérold 086
  8 rue Hérold, 1er
  T 42 33 66 56
  www.rueherold.com

S
Saturne 053
  17 rue Notre-Dame des Victoires, 2e
  T 42 60 31 90
  www.saturne-paris.fr
Septime 052
  80 rue de Charonne, 11e
  T 43 67 38 29
  www.septime-charonne.fr
Le Servan 032
  32 rue Saint-Maur, 11e
  T 55 28 51 82
  www.leservan.com
SÔMA 032
  13 rue de Saintonge, 3e
  T 09 81 82 53 51
Steel Cyclewear & Coffeeshop 043
  58 rue de la Fontaine au Roi, 11e
  T 06 47 58 32 46
Stern Caffè 044
  47 passage des Panoramas, 2e
  T 75 43 63 10
  www.caffestern.com
Sylvestre 039
  Hôtel Thoumieux
  79 rue Saint-Dominique, 7e
  T 47 05 79 79
  www.thoumieux.fr

T
Ten Belles 043
  10 rue de la Grange aux Belles, 10e
  T 42 40 90 78
  www.tenbelles.com
Tour Montparnasse 012
  33 avenue du Maine, 15e
  T 45 38 52 56
  www.tourmontparnasse56.com

Le Train Bleu 096
1st floor
Gare de Lyon
Place Louis Armand, 12ᵉ
T 43 43 09 06
www.le-train-bleu.com
Le Très Particulier 021
Hôtel Particulier Montmartre
23 avenue Junot, 18ᵉ
T 53 41 81 40
www.hotel-particulier-montmartre.com
Triple V 057
5 rue du Mail, 2ᵉ
T 45 84 08 36
www.triple-v.fr

U
UNESCO Headquarters 014
7 place de Fontenoy, 7ᵉ
T 45 68 10 00
www.unesco.org
Until Then 058
77 rue des Rosiers
Saint-Ouen
T 85 58 40 22
www.untilthen.fr
Open from 10am until 6pm,
Friday to Sunday

V
Vallois 064
36 rue de Seine, 6ᵉ
T 46 34 61 07
www.galerie-vallois.com

Verjus 035
52 rue de Richelieu, 1ᵉʳ
T 42 97 54 40
www.verjusparis.com
Villa Besnus 072
85 boulevard de la République
Vaucresson
www.fondationlecorbusier.fr
Villa Savoye 096
82 rue de Villiers
Poissy
T 39 65 01 06
www.villa-savoye.fr

W
Wonmin Park 067
13-15 rue Fernand Forest
Mitry-Mory
www.wonminpark.com

HOTELS

ADDRESSES AND ROOM RATES

Amastan 018
Room rates:
double, from €300
24 rue Jean Mermoz, 8ᵉ
T 49 52 99 70
www.amastanparis.com

Hôtel Bachaumont 017
Room rates:
double, from €200;
Montmartre Suite, from €400;
Loft, from €550
18 rue Bachaumont, 2ᵉ
T 81 66 47 00
www.hotelbachaumont.com

Hôtel Edgar 016
Room rates:
double, from €140
31 rue d'Alexandrie, 2ᵉ
T 40 41 05 19
www.edgarparis.com

Fontevraud L'Hôtel 097
Room rates:
double, from €140
38 rue Saint-Jean de l'Habit
Fontevraud-l'Abbay
Loire Valley
T 02 46 46 10 10
www.fontevraud.fr

Grand Pigalle Hotel 023
Room rates:
double, from €250
29 rue Victor Masse, 9ᵉ
T 85 73 12 00
www.grandpigalle.com

Hôtel Jules & Jim 016
Room rates:
double, from €280
11 rue des Gravilliers, 3ᵉ
T 44 54 13 13
www.hoteljulesetjim.com

Mama Shelter 016
Room rates:
double, from €80
109 rue de Bagnolet, 20ᵉ
T 43 48 48 48
www.mamashelter.com

Hotel Molitor 016
Room rates:
double, from €220
13 rue Nungesser et Coli, 16ᵉ
T 56 07 08 50
www.mltr.fr

Hôtel de Nell 016
Room rates:
double, from €450
7-9 rue du Conservatoire, 9ᵉ
T 44 83 83 60
www.hoteldenell.com

Okko Hotels Nantes Château 096
Room rates:
double, from €125
15 rue de Strasbourg
Nantes
T 02 52 20 00 70
www.okkohotels.com

Hôtel Paradis 016
  Room rates:
  double, from €120
  41 rue des Petites Écuries, 10ᵉ
  T 45 23 08 22
  www.hotelparadisparis.com
Hôtel Particulier Montmartre 021
  Room rates:
  double, from €390;
  Poèmes et Chapeaux Suite, €490;
  Rideau de Cheveux Suite, €590
  23 avenue Junot, 18ᵉ
  T 53 41 81 40
  www.hotel-particulier-montmartre.com
The Peninsula 020
  Room rates:
  double, from €800;
  Historical Suite, price on request
  19 avenue Kléber, 16ᵉ
  T 58 12 28 88
  paris.peninsula.com
Le Pigalle 022
  Room rates:
  double, from €210;
  Pigalle 21, from €290
  9 rue Frochot, 9ᵉ
  T 48 78 37 14
  www.lepigalle.paris
Plaza Athénée 016
  Room rates:
  double, from €850
  25 avenue Montaigne, 8ᵉ
  T 53 67 66 65
  www.dorchestercollection.com

Hôtel Providence 016
  Room rates:
  double, from €190
  90 rue René Boulanger, 10ᵉ
  T 46 34 34 04
  www.hotelprovidenceparis.com
The Ritz 016
  Room rates:
  double, from €900
  15 place Vendôme, 1ᵉʳ
  T 43 16 30 30
  www.ritzparis.com
Hôtel Thoumieux 039
  Room rates:
  double, from €250
  79 rue Saint-Dominique, 7ᵉ
  T 47 05 79 00
  www.thoumieux.fr

WALLPAPER* CITY GUIDES

Executive Editor
Jeremy Case

Author
Alice Cavanagh

City Editor
Belle Place

**Contributing
Photography Editor**
Nabil Butt

Art Editor
Eriko Shimazaki

Junior Editor
Emilee Jane Tombs

Photography Editor
Rebecca Moldenhauer

Contributors
Sophie Dening
Rooksana Hossenally
Catalina L Imizcoz
Sylvia Ugga

Intern
Zoe Wagner

Photo/Digital Assistant
Jade R Arroyo

Production Controller
Nick Seston

Wallpaper*® is a
registered trademark
of Time Inc (UK)

First published 2006
Revised and updated
2008, 2009, 2010, 2011,
2013, 2014 and 2015
Ninth edition 2016

© Phaidon Press Limited

All prices and venue
information are correct at
time of going to press,
but are subject to change.

Original Design
Loran Stosskopf
Map Illustrator
Russell Bell

Contacts
wcg@phaidon.com
@wallpaperguides

More City Guides
www.phaidon.com/travel

Phaidon Press Limited
Regent's Wharf
All Saints Street
London N1 9PA

Phaidon Press Inc
65 Bleecker Street
New York, NY 10012

Phaidon® is a registered
trademark of Phaidon
Press Limited

www.phaidon.com

A CIP Catalogue record for
this book is available from
the British Library.

Printed in China

ISBN 978 0 7148 7241 4

PHOTOGRAPHERS

Martin Argyroglo
Le Château, pp102-103

Pol Baril
L'Institut Guerlain,
pp094-095

Luc Boegly
Créteil Cathédrale,
p100, p101

Marcin Brzezicki
Maison de Verre, p077

Raffaele Cipolletta
Department of Islamic Art,
pp028-029

Adrien Dirand
Monsieur Bleu, p027
La Buvette, p048
Balmain, p088

Charles Duprat
Galerie Thaddaeus Ropac,
p066

Todd Eberle
Fondation Louis Vuitton,
pp060-061

Julien Fernandez
Paris city view,
inside front cover
Centre Pompidou,
pp010-011
Hôtel Bachaumont, p017
Amastan, pp018-019
Le Pigalle, p022, p023
The Broken Arm, p025
Clover, p030
Gravity Bar, p031
52 Faubourg Saint Denis,
p033
Ellsworth, p034, p035
Dersou, pp036-037
Restaurant Guy Savoy,
p038
Restaurant Yam'Tcha,
p040, p041
Caillebotte, p042
Café Oberkampf, p043
Stern Caffè, p044
Café Kitsuné, p045
Le Mary Celeste, p049
Clamato, pp050-051
Charlotte de Tonnac and
Hugo Sauzay, p055
Until Then, p058, p059
Galerie des Galeries, p062
Galerie Allen, p063
Philharmonie de Paris,
pp074-075

Fondation Jérôme
Seydoux-Pathé, p076
Officine Universelle Buly,
p085
Rue Hérold, pp086-087
Boutique Alaïa, p092, p093

Jérôme Galland
Saturne, p053

Clément Guillaume
Septime, p052
Communist Party
Headquarters, pp078-079
Nose, p089

Alex Hill
Hôtel Particulier
Montmartre, p021

Hotelexistence.com
Grande Arche de la
Défense, p013
UNESCO Headquarters,
pp014-015

Olivier Martin-Gambier
Maison La Roche, p073

Nicolas Mathéus
Fontevraud L'Hôtel, p097

Florent Michel
Palais de Tokyo, p026

Emile Ouroumov
Vallois, pp064-065

Jean Etienne Portail
Paco Rabanne, p081

James Reeve
Brasserie Thoumieux, p039

Studio Bouroullec
Lustre Gabriel, p068

Casper Sejersen
Robert Stadler, p057

Hisao Suzuki
Louvre-Lens, pp098-099

PARIS

A COLOUR-CODED GUIDE TO THE CITY'S HOT 'HOODS

MONTMARTRE/PIGALLE

The hill is the haunt of the *haute* bourgeoisie; at its foot is the city's (reformed) sin central

CANAL SAINT-MARTIN

Alongside this canal in the 10th arrondissement, east Paris hipsters set up shop and play

CHAMPS-ÉLYSÉES

Les Champs will always be touristy, but the area around it is full of stylish destinations

RÉPUBLIQUE/BASTILLE

Young at heart but more polished these days, thanks to a shot of *bon chic, bon genre*

MARAIS

These streets were made for strolling. Galleries, boutiques, bars, bistros – take your pick

BEAUBOURG/LOUVRE

Come here for art and architecture that is impossible to ignore and still apt to inspire

SAINT-GERMAIN-DES-PRÉS/QUARTIER LATIN

Sartre and de Beauvoir's Left Bank stomping ground is more about retail these days

LES INVALIDES

Among the layers of history is Jean Nouvel's home for the museum of non-Western art

For a full description of each neighbourhood, see the Introduction.
Featured venues are colour-coded, according to the district in which they are located.